CLIMATE WARRIORS

Fourteen Scientists and Fourteen Ways We Can Save Our Planet

LAURA GEHL

M Millbrook Press / Minneapolis

For all of the kids and all of the scientists who are working together, in big and small ways, to save our planet

Acknowledgments
Writing about climate change is a daunting task, but many people helped me make this book the best it could be. The list includes Sam Bliss, Hena Khan, Ann McCallum Staats, and Joan Waites, who read and improved my drafts; the amazing team at Lerner, especially Jesseca Fusco, Kimberly Morales, Erica Johnson, Danielle Carnito, Giliane Mansfeldt, Lillian Dondero, and Carol Hinz; and my incomparable agent Erzsi Deàk, whose faith in me and my writing never wavers. Most of all, I would like to thank the fourteen scientists featured in these pages, who took the time to help me understand their important work: Jessi Allen, Shahzeen Attari, Wendy Chou, Ric Colacito, Tom Crowther, Natasha DeJarnett, Ryan Emanuel, Mark Jacobson, Sossina Haile, Meg Holden, David Rolnick, Natalie Rubio, Corinne Scown, and Lisa Windham-Myers.

Millbrook Press™
An imprint of Lerner Publishing Group, Inc.
241 First Avenue North
Minneapolis, MN 55401 USA

For reading levels and more information, look up this title at www.lernerbooks.com.

Diagram on page 11 by Laura K. Westlund.

Designed by Kimberly Morales.
Main body text set in Univers LT Std. Typeface provided by Adobe Systems.

Library of Congress Cataloging-in-Publication Data

Names: Gehl, Laura, author.
Title: Climate warriors: fourteen scientists and fourteen ways we can save our planet / by Laura Gehl.
Description: Minneapolis: Millbrook Press, [2023] | Includes bibliographical references and index. |
    Audience: Ages 9–14 | Audience: Grades 4–6 | Summary: "Meet fourteen scientists working to combat
    climate change—in fourteen different ways. This book informs young readers and gives them the tools
    they need to make a difference"—Provided by publisher.
Identifiers: LCCN 2022020281 (print) | LCCN 2022020282 (ebook) | ISBN 9781728460406 (library binding) |
    ISBN 9781728485706 (ebook)
Subjects: LCSH: Climate change mitigation—Juvenile literature. | Climatic changes—Juvenile literature.
Classification: LCC TD171.75. G44 2023 (print) | LCC TD171.75 (ebook) | DDC 363.738/74—dc23/eng/20220722

LC record available at https://lccn.loc.gov/2022020281
LC ebook record available at https://lccn.loc.gov/2022020282

Manufactured in the United States of America
1-51507-50379-10/10/2022

CONTENTS

INTRODUCTION TO CLIMATE CHANGE

In Florida, Elena's family prepares to evacuate their home for the second time in two months as a hurricane approaches the coast. In California, Josh breathes in smoky air from wildfires many miles away when he goes outside to play soccer. In West Virginia, Sara's school bus has to take a new route, because recent flooding caused a landslide that has blocked the usual road.

Elena, Josh, and Sara live in a world with an increasing number of wildfires, droughts, heat waves, intense hurricanes, and floods. In their world, glaciers are melting. Sea levels are rising. Animal and plant species face extinction. Disease outbreaks shut down entire countries. Unfortunately, their world is also our world. And not our world in the future but our world right now. Climate change is already causing our planet to transform in scary ways.

Sometimes, when something is big and frightening, we don't want to think about it. Climate change is the biggest problem humans have ever faced. So it's not surprising that both kids and adults get overwhelmed. It's easy to feel as though nothing we do will make a difference. When I started writing this book, I talked to scientists who believe we *can* fight climate change, especially if we work together. Talking to those fourteen scientists gave me hope and resolve—hope, because smart, caring, dedicated people are working on the problem of climate change from so many different angles; and resolve to do my part. Now I want to share my own hope and resolve with you. In this book, you'll read about many things we can do to slow down climate change. And they all start with the same first step: *don't give up!*

WHAT IS CLIMATE CHANGE?

Let's start with what *climate* means. Climate is the weather patterns in a certain place over a long period of time. One way to understand the difference between climate and weather is by thinking about clothes. The climate tells you which types of clothes to buy so that you can be comfortable where you live over the course of the entire year (more hoodies in Alaska, more shorts in Florida), and the weather tells you which clothes to wear on a specific day (even in sunny Florida, some days call for a sweatshirt and pants). Climate includes the average temperature in a certain place as well as the amount of rain and snow that fall each year. So *climate change* is when there is a change in the average temperature, rain, or snowfall in a certain place, or a combination of these.

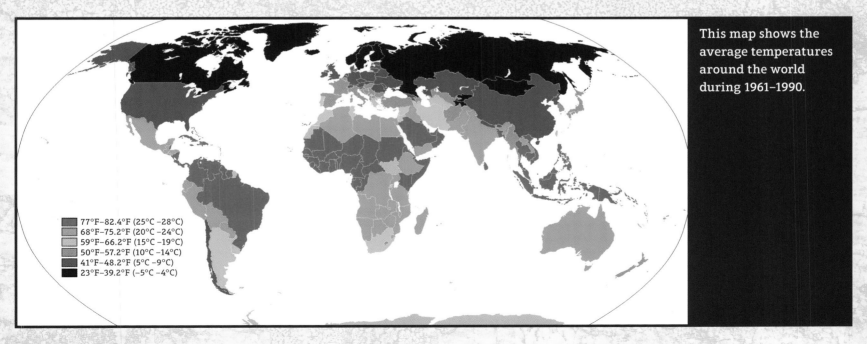

Legend:
- 77°F–82.4°F (25°C –28°C)
- 68°F–75.2°F (20°C –24°C)
- 59°F–66.2°F (15°C –19°C)
- 50°F–57.2°F (10°C –14°C)
- 41°F–48.2°F (5°C –9°C)
- 23°F–39.2°F (–5°C –4°C)

This map shows the average temperatures around the world during 1961–1990.

Throughout Earth's history, the climate has changed drastically. Our planet has experienced extremely warm periods and at least five ice ages! What caused these drastic changes? Many different things—volcanic activity, meteorite impacts, variations in Earth's orbit, and more. But when we talk about *climate change* now, there are two big differences from these earlier variations in climate. First, in the past, the climate has typically changed slowly, over tens of thousands or millions of years. Today, the climate is changing much faster. Second, the natural factors that caused earlier changes are *not* the cause of the climate change happening now. The leading cause of climate change now is us—humans.

HOW ARE HUMANS CAUSING CLIMATE CHANGE?

You may have heard of the *greenhouse effect*. This term refers to the way gases in Earth's atmosphere trap the sun's heat, just as the walls and roof of a greenhouse hold in heat to help plants grow. The greenhouse effect is good because the trapped heat makes Earth warm enough for us to live. On the moon, where there is no greenhouse effect, nighttime temperatures are about 200°F (111°C) colder than the freezer where you keep your ice cream! But human activities are releasing more and more greenhouse gases, including carbon dioxide and methane, into the atmosphere. And this is *not* good.

When power plants burn fossil fuels such as coal and natural gas to make electricity for our lights, computers, and cell phones, they release carbon dioxide into the atmosphere. The same thing happens when we drive cars or fly in planes that use fossil fuels. But burning fossil fuels is only one of several ways that humans are causing increased greenhouse gas emissions. As trees grow, they take in carbon dioxide through the process of photosynthesis and store that carbon in their trunks, branches, leaves, and roots. When we cut down forests, the stored carbon dioxide goes

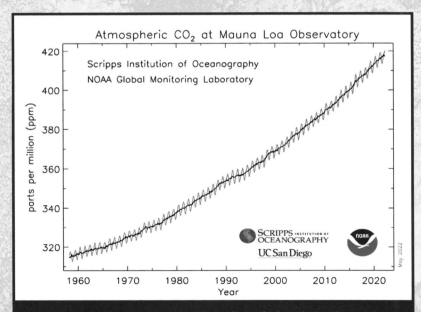

Over the past sixty years, carbon dioxide levels in the atmosphere have continued to rise. This graph shows the increase of carbon dioxide in the atmosphere from 1960–2020 at Mauna Loa Observatory in Waimea, Hawaii.

back into the atmosphere. And when we bury huge piles of trash—discarded food, outgrown clothes, old toys—it causes greenhouse gas emissions too. A giant trash dump is called a landfill, and bacteria in landfills gradually break down the waste. This produces large quantities of methane, which is released into the atmosphere.

As human activities emit more greenhouse gases into the atmosphere, more of the sun's heat is trapped by those gases—just as an actual greenhouse traps the sun's heat to help plants grow—and the average temperature on Earth increases. This phenomenon is called *global warming*, and it is leading to problems around the world. As temperatures rise, glaciers melt, contributing to rising sea levels and increased flooding. Higher temperatures also increase evaporation of moisture from soil and bodies of water. This evaporation leads to droughts in traditionally drier areas. Meanwhile, increased moisture in the air generates heavier rain and snow in other locations. The combination of warmer, moister air and warmer ocean water also fuels hurricanes, increasing their intensity.

WHAT CAN WE DO?

Have you ever read a choose-your-own-path book, where some choices lead to escape from killer robots or an erupting volcano, while other choices

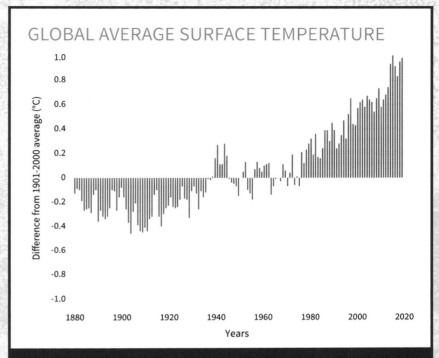

GLOBAL AVERAGE SURFACE TEMPERATURE

Earth's average surface temperature has increased by a little more than 1.8°F (1°C) since 1880. This sounds small, but it's a very big change, according to climate scientists.

lead to increased danger? Just as those books include many options to escape from peril, we have many ways to slow down climate change and to limit the effects of climate change on humans and other species. Decreasing carbon emissions, the amount of carbon dioxide we release into the atmosphere by burning fossil fuels, is very important. One way we can decrease emissions is by encouraging businesses and individual people to reduce their carbon footprint, the amount of carbon released into the atmosphere because of their actions. For example, a company can stop stocking its cafeteria with single-use plastics, and an individual can bike instead of driving. But there are numerous other paths people can take to approach the huge problem of climate change.

In the following pages, you'll meet fourteen scientists. I call them Climate Warriors because they are using their intelligence, education, skills, and determination to fight climate change in fourteen different ways. To guide their work, all of these scientists ask big questions. Their questions include How can humans live comfortably without increasing greenhouse gases? and How can we take extra carbon dioxide out of the atmosphere? To answer these big questions, the scientists conduct research, designing specific projects and experiments to give them more information. For example, some scientists find options for people to heat and cool their homes or get from one

place to another without burning fossil fuels. Other scientists explore ways to remove carbon from the atmosphere, such as planting trees to restore healthy forests.

Scientists also help fight climate change by collecting and publishing scientific data. Lawmakers can use this data to make decisions about which laws we need in order to slow down climate change. Teachers and writers can share data to spread the word about how to fight climate

Thousands of students joined the School Strike for Climate in New York City in 2022. Youth activist Greta Thunberg started this movement in her home country of Sweden in 2018.

change. Activists may use scientific data to persuade companies to adopt more climate-friendly policies and to push elected officials to pass more climate-friendly laws. Individual people like you and me can use scientific data to make good choices about what to eat, what to buy, and how to heat our homes. Some choices result in more greenhouse gases being released into the atmosphere than others. With the help of accurate information, everyone can make the best decisions to combat climate change.

As you read this book, you'll see many paths that you yourself can choose to help flight climate change. Maybe you will stop using plastic sandwich bags or make yourself meatless lunches. Maybe you will plant trees in your community or collect rainwater for your garden. Maybe you will

Yikes! What Does That Word Mean?

When you are reading about each Climate Warrior, you will see words in blue. These words will help you understand that specific scientist's work. The blue words are defined in black boxes in each scientist's section of the book. You can find additional words that will help you understand climate change defined in the glossary in the back of the book.

give a speech at your school to educate others about climate change or write to your elected officials asking them to pass climate-friendly laws. Whichever path you choose, you can be a Climate Warrior too.

TOM CROWTHER

Growing up in Wales, in the United Kingdom, Tom Crowther says he was "an absolute nature addict." He had no interest in cartoons on TV. Instead, he spent his time searching for lizards and snakes outside. In fact, Tom loved snakes so much that he considered studying them as his job. But when Tom found out that studying snakes involves taking blood samples with needles, which hurts the snakes, he decided he would "study what keeps the snakes alive" instead. Today, Tom is an ecologist who researches forest ecosystems, *biodiversity*, and how all life on Earth is connected.

One of the big questions Tom looks at is this: How can we restore forests around the world?

For Tom, fighting climate change comes down to feedback loops. Climate change itself is driven by feedback loops that work like this: Humans are causing more carbon emissions to go into the air. More carbon in the air means higher temperatures. And higher temperatures cause more carbon to come out of the soil, leading to even higher temperatures. And so on. This is one of many damaging feedback loops that are starting because of human activity. The good news is we can also create feedback loops to *fight* climate change.

Tom sees reforestation, which means allowing trees to regrow in areas where forests were cut down, as a way to partially reverse the damage humans have caused to Earth's environment. If we can successfully restore forests around the world, those forests could help remove extra carbon from our atmosphere. This is because plants take in carbon dioxide in order to make their own food through a process called photosynthesis. The carbon is then stored within the plants and the soils below them. Tom believes ecosystem restoration could pull up to 30 percent of the extra carbon dioxide—which is hundreds of billions of tons—out of the atmosphere.

BIODIVERSITY: the variety of life in a certain ecosystem or in the world

What Is a Feedback Loop?

A feedback loop is when one action causes another action that then affects the first action. If you like to dance, then you will dance more. Because you dance more, you improve at dancing, and people might compliment you on your dancing. That makes you like dancing even more than before, and so you dance even more, and you get even better at dancing. This is an example of a feedback loop.

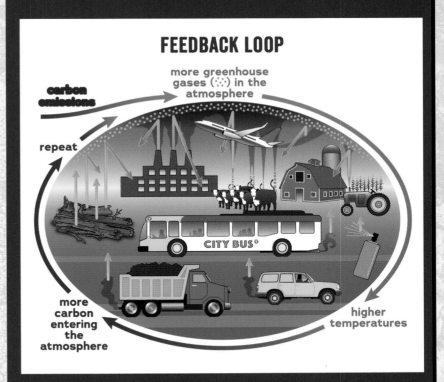

FEEDBACK LOOP

carbon emissions

more greenhouse gases (∴) in the atmosphere

repeat

CITY BUS

more carbon entering the atmosphere

higher temperatures

Climate change is driven by feedback loops like this one. Vehicles and deforestation, factories and farms, and even aerosol cans contribute to greenhouse gases in the atmosphere.

The key to success in restoration, Tom says, is creating feedback loops that have positive outcomes. Over one billion people around the world drink coffee regularly. In the United States alone, people drink millions of cups of coffee every day! Unfortunately, all that coffee comes at a big cost to the environment. Coffee production usually involves cutting down trees to clear space to grow the coffee plants. To make matters worse, after several years without trees, the soil no longer contains the nutrients and water that are needed for optimal coffee growth. This means that farmers need fertilizers and watering systems to keep their coffee plants growing. But Tom and his colleagues have been learning from farms that work with nature to keep the entire system more sustainable.

One coffee farm in Ethiopia decided not to cut down the forest at all. They planted coffee trees within the sunny patches of the rain forest. The rain forest captures the water and nutrients that the coffee plants need. The coffee trees have grown very well, and the farm has actually made more money than other coffee farms because they don't need to pay for fertilizers and watering systems. Now other farmers in the area are letting trees recover so *their* coffee farms can be more productive too. The choice to restore forests is spreading from farm to farm, benefiting both nature and the farmers.

"The climate change feedback loop is out of control and scary. But at the same time, we can start our own feedback loops that can also grow to incredible potential."

Tom loves seeing salamanders and other small creatures in forests. They are signs of a healthy ecosystem.

When we restore forests, more plants are available to take carbon out of the atmosphere, which is valuable for fighting climate change. But, as Tom explains, that's not the only benefit. An important part of helping our planet is increasing biodiversity. Restoring forests means more insects, birds, and animals, and this creates another feedback loop. A healthy ecosystem with a lot of biodiversity supports all the species in that ecosystem and can exist indefinitely. Tom says, "The more biodiversity we have in our global ecosystem, the more sustainable it is for supporting human life."

RECOMMENDATIONS FROM TOM'S WORK

We need to create feedback loops by supporting local nature conservation and restoration efforts. If a local community finds a way to make money from healthy ecosystems, they will be motivated to keep protecting them. One way governments can help is by providing money to support new and expanding projects. For example, farmers might be willing to plant apple orchards instead of using their land to raise cows. The apple trees would pull carbon dioxide out of the atmosphere and store it as they grow, and fewer cows raised for food means less methane produced by animals burping and passing gas. But it could take ten years before the apple trees grow big enough for the farmers to make money

selling apples. The government could give the farmers money during that time, and then after ten years, the orchards will be profitable on their own.

WHAT *YOU* CAN DO

Tom says, "You can be the start of your own feedback loop." If you are interested in biodiversity, you can find a way to help increase it. The more you work on increasing biodiversity, the more your friends will become interested in biodiversity. The more interested your friends become, the more they will participate. As the cycle continues, you will increase the positive effects of biodiversity for the planet. So how can you help increase biodiversity? One way is by "rewilding" a garden on your balcony, in your backyard, or in your community. Rewilding a space means encouraging plants to grow that would have naturally grown in your area before humans lived there. These are also called native plants. Rewilded gardens do not need chemicals such as fertilizers and pest repellent in order to grow and thrive, and they attract insects, birds, and animals, increasing the biodiversity of the area. You can find native plants for your area, and see what birds they will attract, here: www.audubon.org/native-plants.

Making Cities More Climate-Friendly
MEG HOLDEN

Meg Holden didn't grow up in a city. But after attending college on Vancouver Island, Canada, where she spent time in beautiful forests, Meg realized most people didn't have "the magic of forests in their daily lives." She moved to New York City for graduate school, excited to find out what people loved about cities. Meg wanted to combine her passion for the environment with learning how cities are planned, how they grow, and how they change over time. She became an expert in **urban studies**, focusing on how cities can benefit both the people who live there and the planet.

One of the big questions Meg works on is this: How can we make cities more sustainable so that we can meet our needs while also making sure future generations will be able to meet their needs?

Meg points to greater walkability as one idea that has successfully increased sustainability in cities around the world, while also meeting the needs of city residents. By taking space originally designed for vehicles and turning it into walkable space, we can reduce pollution and energy use in cities, which is great for the planet. And Meg says increasing walkable areas in cities leads to spaces that work for recreation, markets, parades, protests,

URBAN STUDIES: the study of cities and the behavior of people in cities

Meg evaluates the work of student architects who are learning to design sustainable neighborhoods.

"Cities played a big role in getting us into the mess we are in with climate change. Thankfully, cities also give us key ideas for getting out of the mess."

and more, meeting a variety of different needs. Some scientific studies show that people are also happier in more walkable cities!

Meg has studied urban neighborhoods that were built to be models of sustainable design. She and her colleagues found that model cities around the globe have similarities. For example, model neighborhoods on several different continents have buildings about eight stories tall, rather than towering skyscrapers. These eight-story buildings are tall enough to fit a lot of residents but not so tall that people on the top floor feel disconnected from the city below. Many of the model cities also have central courtyards in their buildings. Courtyards provide kids a safe place to play outside, allow space for plants and trees, and create a sense of connectedness between neighbors. A third common idea was including ways to collect rainwater. This water can be used for flushing toilets, washing clothes, watering plants, and more.

A Model Sustainable Neighborhood Built for the Olympics

In 2010, Vancouver, Canada, where Meg lives, hosted the Olympic Games. The city built the Olympic Village as a model sustainable neighborhood. City planners designed the neighborhood to be entirely walkable, with lots of trees. The neighborhood's community center harvests rainwater for flushing toilets and uses solar energy to power its lights and other electronics. The neighborhood also uses waste heat, the heat left over when you use hot water in your shower or washing machine, as a source of power. More than ten years after the Olympics, the athletes are long gone, but regular people enjoy living in this sustainable neighborhood, which has been studied by city planners around the world. Unfortunately, the Olympic Village is an expensive place to live. Meg says that affordability needs to be part of the conversation every time a sustainable neighborhood is built so that living in this type of community is accessible for everyone.

New technologies, such as electric buses and sensors that reduce energy use in office buildings, are important for making cities more sustainable. However, Meg believes the most important piece of the puzzle is conversations about how people live in their neighborhoods. People who live in cities have a variety of backgrounds, incomes, and needs. An elderly person living alone does not have the same needs as a family with three young children. Meg says the biggest successes start when city planners "engage real people in conversation about why it matters to make cities more sustainable" and when you can find ways to meet the needs of different groups in a sustainable way.

RECOMMENDATIONS FROM MEG'S WORK

Meg says the largest emissions reductions in cities will come from changing the way land is used. We need to make cities more walkable, include more green spaces, and build better public transportation systems. We also need updated building codes that require new buildings to use renewable energy. All new buildings should also be airtight. Airtight

"How can we remake our cities so that they do not destabilize the climate?"

buildings prevent heat loss in the winter and block summer heat from getting in, which means these buildings don't need to use as much energy for heating or cooling.

WHAT *YOU* CAN DO

Saving water helps fight climate change because it takes a lot of energy to pump, clean, and deliver water to your home. Instead of using clean drinkable water for all of your daily tasks, you can collect rainwater by putting a container at the bottom of a gutter or by placing a container on a lawn or an apartment building rooftop. Don't drink the water you collect. Instead, use it for other things, such as watering plants or washing muddy shoes. You can also save the water that is left over after you boil pasta or eggs and use it for making soup or bread. And you can save water by taking shorter showers and turning off the tap while you are brushing your teeth.

WENDY CHOU

Wendy Chou enjoyed spending time outdoors as a kid, but she had no idea she would grow up to work on the problem of climate change. In fact, Wendy didn't learn about global warming or climate change when she was in elementary school. She contrasts her own childhood with her young son's, noting that he is already aware of climate change and the need for everyone to work together on this global issue. In college, Wendy took a class on climate change that had a dramatic impact on her life. She was drawn to the subject because she could see that it was something very big, and very important, affecting a huge number of people. She remembers thinking, "I really want to learn more and help solve this problem."

Wendy went on to study environmental science and **public policy** in both college and graduate school. Now, she uses the skills she learned to help spread the word about climate change to policy makers and community members.

As a **climate communicator**, one big question Wendy focuses on in her work is this: What messages can we share to make people act on climate change?

In her job working for an environmental organization, Wendy uses websites, email, and social media to reach out to people in her community. She takes up-to-date information about climate change impacts and solutions from researchers and rewrites it in less complicated language. This way everyone, not just scientists, can understand the material. She helps people learn why eating less meat and driving an electric car can decrease their carbon footprint. Wendy wants to communicate that when it comes to fighting climate change, "everyone can be doing something."

Another message Wendy strives to share is that making changes is easier when we work together. She invites people to events that her organization hosts so that they can learn from experts and from one another about solutions for climate change. Some events are for business leaders. If one business has an idea about how to reduce food waste or use less plastic, other business leaders can hear about the method and maybe try it themselves. Wendy and her coworkers also bring people together for a Meatless May Challenge. It can be really hard to make a change from eating meat most days to eating less meat for a whole month or more. But it is easier when you try the challenge with other people. Local restaurants join the effort by offering special deals for participants. New participants can ask to be paired with a buddy who is used to making vegetarian choices. The buddy can share meatless recipes and offer encouragement.

Wendy also communicates a third message: that fighting climate change can be good for the environment *and* for your budget. For example, in many places, heating and cooling your home is necessary for you to be comfortable. But furnaces and air conditioners use a lot of energy. Wendy teaches people about the electric heat pump, a device that can both heat and cool your home while using less energy than a furnace and air conditioner. Wendy also shows people how they can get money back from their local government if they buy a heat pump, or another energy-efficient item, such as an electric car. Certain government programs make energy-saving items less expensive so that more people can contribute to fighting climate change. Wendy says, "Sometimes people equate environmentalism with sacrifice. But it doesn't have to be a sacrifice."

Wendy's team works together to share ways everyone can take action to combat climate change.

RECOMMENDATIONS FROM WENDY'S WORK

Individual efforts add up, and everyone can help fight climate change. It is easier for individuals to make beneficial choices for the environment when they do it together. Wendy points out that change can be a "domino effect." When one person makes a choice that helps the environment, such as using solar power or beginning Meatless Mondays, then a friend or neighbor might notice the change and decide to do the same thing. The domino effect can apply to businesses too!

WHAT *YOU* CAN DO

Consider forming or joining a green team or an environmental club at your school. You can talk to your school leaders about how to provide meatless options in the cafeteria or reduce single-use plastics. Outside of her job, Wendy and her friends started a podcast to talk about solutions to climate change. You and your classmates could start a podcast too! Whatever you decide to do as a team, Wendy says, "It is easier to do things together than by yourself."

"We want to change people's thoughts about what 'normal' is. Maybe we can make it a bit less 'normal' to celebrate certain holidays by eating lots of meat."

Why Does Eating Less Meat Help Fight Climate Change?

Approximately nine out of ten people in the United States eat meat. Unfortunately, raising animals for meat, especially cows and sheep, can contribute to climate change in a few ways. First, farmers may destroy forests in order to have land for their animals, which releases all the carbon stored in the forests into the air. Second, cows and sheep produce methane by burping and passing gas. Remember, carbon dioxide and methane are greenhouse gases, which means they trap heat in the atmosphere and contribute to climate change. Because we raise many, many cows and sheep so we can have beef and lamb, the gas the animals produce adds up to a LOT of extra methane in the atmosphere. And methane is a much more powerful greenhouse gas than carbon dioxide. Chickens and pigs do not produce as much methane as cows and sheep, but poultry and pork farms still contribute to climate change. Even if people do not want to switch to a 100 percent plant-based (vegan) diet, if everyone eats a little less meat, it can add up to a huge decrease in greenhouse gas emissions.

Protecting Lichens from Climate Change
JESSI ALLEN

As a child, Jessi Allen loved horses. In addition to riding them, she spent hours thinking about different types of horses and grouping them by breed and color. Little did Jessi know that she would grow up to use that same kind of thinking as a conservation biologist. Now, instead of horses, Jessi studies lichens. Part of her work is classifying lichens, which means grouping them into categories just as she did with horses years ago.

One of the big questions Jessi studies is this: How can we protect lichens from extinction in the face of climate change?

As people walk around in their daily lives, they may not notice the lichens on sidewalks or trees. But lichens perform many important jobs. Lichens produce more than one thousand chemicals, including some that are used to make medicines. Lichens provide shelter for tiny organisms, nesting material for hummingbirds, and food for reindeer and other animals. Unfortunately, some lichen species are in danger of extinction. While thousands of plants and animals are on the US government's endangered species list, the list includes only two lichens. This means that many other endangered lichen species don't receive the same protection that these species do.

All living things on Earth are connected. In order for humans to have clean air to breathe and food

Lichens can grow on natural surfaces such as bark, rock, and stone, as well as human-made surfaces such as metal, plastic, and cloth.

to eat, a wide variety of animals, plants, fungi, and microorganisms need to exist. As Arctic areas grow warmer due to climate change, lichens in those areas may be in danger. As rising sea levels cause salt water to flow into swampy coastal areas, lichens there may face peril too. If these lichen species go extinct, it could lead to other species going extinct as well.

After observing that climate change threatens communities of lichens, Jessi and other scientists are investigating ways to help the lichens move to safer locations. Lichen species are able to move gradually over time by themselves. However, with conditions shifting so fast due to climate change, lichens may need human help with moving. For example, Jessi moved a number of lichens from a swamp area where rising sea levels had caused salt water to invade their homes. The lichens would have died without her help. Moving lichens is not easy, however. Jessi has to pick up lichens with tweezers, transport them to a new location, and then use a special type of glue to stick the lichens onto their new homes. Jessi has also tried stapling lichens onto trees, which "worked pretty darn well," she says. Another way Jessi has helped lichens adjust to new tree homes was by making what she calls "lichen Christmas ornaments." She glued the lichens to loops of fishing line and hung the loops from tree branches. Eventually, the lichens transferred to the tree and grew there on their own. "You get to be really creative with problem-solving," Jessi says.

RECOMMENDATIONS FROM JESSI'S WORK

For lichens and other species threatened by climate change, Jessi says, "conservation corridors are essential." Like a hallway connecting two rooms of

"Lichens perform so many really essential ecosystem services."

a school, a conservation corridor is a pathway that connects two natural areas. The corridor is a strip of wildlife habitat that provides a safe place for all species, from lichens to larger plants and animals, to travel from one protected area to another as needed. Jessi says we must establish north-south corridors

Symbiosis

Lichens can look similar to moss, which is a plant. But lichens are not like moss or like any other plant, animal, or fungus! Lichens are made up of two organisms, a fungus and an alga, functioning together. (You might not have heard the word *alga* before, but you may have heard of algae, which is the plural form of alga. Many seaweeds are types of algae.) The fungus and the alga are an example of symbiosis—when two organisms of different species live close together and interact. The alga helps the fungus by making food through photosynthesis, like most plants. The fungus protects the alga and anchors it to a rock or tree. Through symbiosis, lichens can live in places where most other organisms cannot survive. Lichens can grow on the tops of mountains, in deserts, and even on a sidewalk in New York City.

and east-west corridors so that species can move in any direction without encountering busy roads or other human obstacles. She says, "As species are migrating, they need someplace to go."

WHAT *YOU* CAN DO

Jessi says, "Anyone can collect data on what species are around" and "It's always valuable to have more data." As our climate continues to change, this data helps Jessi and other scientists see how lichens are moving over time. By keeping track of lichens, scientists will be ready to jump in and help with relocating lichen communities if needed. If you notice lichens where you live, you can use iNaturalist (https://www.inaturalist.org/) to share what you find with scientists and other people who care about nature.

"Our most famous lichen-eaters are the reindeer, which are completely dependent on lichen. They eat lichen all year-round."

Lichens exist in many different colors, including red, orange, yellow, green, black, brown, and gray.

Using AI to Fight Climate Change
DAVID ROLNICK

People who knew David Rolnick when he was younger probably wouldn't have predicted he would grow up to work on **artificial intelligence (AI)**. While David had a long list of childhood passions—math, music, reading, birds, insects—computers didn't even make the list. But after college, David's love of math led him to AI. He explains that AI is about finding patterns. You give a computer large amounts of data, and it learns to find patterns. David says, "The computer can find patterns far faster than a person, and it doesn't get bored, so it can look at a lot of data."

One big question David considers is this: How can artificial intelligence help us fight climate change?

Working with experts in energy, transportation, climate science, and other areas, David has discovered a range of ways that AI can assist in combating climate change. For example, AI can analyze photos from satellites and figure out where forests are being destroyed or which coastal areas are at most risk of flooding. AI can also monitor energy use in office buildings, automatically adjusting lights and temperatures in different rooms, depending on when and where people are working, which can significantly reduce energy use.

ARTIFICIAL INTELLIGENCE (AI):
computer systems capable of performing tasks such as recommendations and predictions

David studies how AI can improve electrical grids. Using renewable energy sources such as solar and wind power is better than using energy from power plants that burn fossil fuels, but the amount of power we can collect from the sun or wind changes with the weather and time of day. AI can help electrical grids become more efficient by calculating how much total power is needed, how much power we can get from renewable sources, and how much power should be generated by power plants on a minute-to-minute basis.

David warns that we can't hand the problem of climate change over to a computer and say, "Solve it!" Computers solve problems fast, but only very specific problems and only if humans give them the right data and ask the right questions. He explains, "AI can sometimes help for some problems, but only if you work together with the people who really understand those problems, whether those people are in electricity or transportation or land use."

RECOMMENDATIONS FROM DAVID'S WORK

Fighting climate change is a team effort. It requires scientists and experts with different knowledge and skills to work together. Experts in artificial intelligence can help experts in other areas solve problems related to climate change. However, collaboration is essential, because AI can only solve problems if it receives all the right data from people who are knowledgeable about other areas, such as renewable energy or forestry.

WHAT *YOU* CAN DO

David says he uses AI to help fight climate change because that's what he is good at. But he points out that everyone has different skills, and people can help in lots of ways. What are your skills? If you enjoy writing, you could write to your local officials about ways your community could use less energy from fossil fuels. If you like public speaking, you could share your ideas at a city council meeting. If you are good at coding, you could create a game that teaches other kids about climate change.

How Does AI Work?

AI uses computers to do things the human mind usually does, such as solving problems and making decisions. One example of AI is when a TV streaming service suggests new shows based on shows you've watched. If you watch cooking shows, AI might suggest a show called *Next Great Baking Boss*. And when you play chess against a computer, you are actually playing against AI. Computers can look at lots of information and find patterns much faster than humans. However, computers cannot think creatively the way we can. When people talk about a branch of AI called *machine learning*, it means that computers use lots of data to gradually improve their accuracy in making simple decisions. For example, if a computer is given lots of cat pictures and lots of dog pictures, it can learn to analyze a new photo and say if it is of a cat or a dog.

LISA WINDHAM-MYERS

Growing up, Lisa Windham-Myers always picked indoor chores such as setting the table over outdoor chores such as yardwork because she hated getting dirty. She liked playing piano, swimming, and doing math—activities where she could stay clean. Nobody would have expected Lisa to become an ecologist who spends much of her time stomping through **wetlands** and collecting soil samples. Lisa says, "It's so weird to my whole family that I'm always muddy now."

One of the big questions Lisa tries to answer is this: How can we measure and protect blue carbon?

WETLANDS: places where water covers the soil or where there is a lot of water near the surface of the soil. Marshes, bogs, and swamps are types of wetlands.

Blue carbon is what scientists call the carbon stored in coastal and ocean ecosystems. Along coastlines, wetland plants pull carbon out of the air. That carbon is stored in the plants and in the soil. This is a natural way to reduce the amount of carbon dioxide in the atmosphere. Forests also remove carbon from the air and store it, but wetlands pull carbon out faster and hold the carbon in soil for longer than forests do.

When coastal ecosystems are disrupted, such as when developers destroy a wetland to build a hotel, two things happen. First, lots of carbon is released back into the air, where it contributes to climate change. Second, the developed area is at increased danger of flooding. Coastal ecosystems protect land from flooding during severe weather, and we lose that protection when we destroy wetlands.

When a forest is destroyed, we can see the damage from satellites. Wetlands, on the other hand, are often much smaller, and their carbon is mostly stored underground rather than in the trunks and leaves of trees. This means the carbon-storing benefits of wetlands cannot be seen as easily from above. As a result, governments have not focused on protecting wetlands as much as protecting forests. A lot of computer models that analyze various factors affecting our changing climate also ignore wetlands.

Lisa and her colleagues work to measure blue carbon. These scientists want people to understand the trade-offs when they are making decisions about coastal lands. Lisa explains that after the last ice age, sea levels rose as glaciers melted. But once the sea level stopped rising, about eight thousand years ago, carbon began building up in wetlands. When a marsh is drained to use the land for farming, all the stored carbon is released into the air, where it contributes to climate change. Lisa explains, "You've now lost eight thousand years of carbon. That's a long-term loss for a short-term gain."

Lisa says that we need to recognize the value of coastal lands so that we do not lose them. While people who love to fish may know that wetlands are good for fishing, and people who enjoy bird-watching may want to protect the birds who live in wetlands, we must also understand how vital these lands are from a climate change perspective. Lisa stresses that these wetlands ecosystems are "a natural climate solution where nobody has to do anything . . . it just keeps going if you leave it alone."

RECOMMENDATIONS FROM LISA'S WORK

Conserving coastal ecosystems is an excellent way to fight climate change. We need to prioritize conserving coastal ecosystems the same way we prioritize protecting forests. This means including coastal ecosystems in computer climate models and the carbon market (see sidebar on page 31) and making sure government protections for forests worldwide are extended to wetlands as well.

WHAT *YOU* CAN DO

The soil in wetlands holds more carbon than most soil because it is largely underwater. Under water, plant material breaks down very slowly, allowing carbon to stay in the soil instead of going back into the air. If you have a backyard, you can help increase the amount of carbon in your own soil by composting. Composting is putting items such as eggshells, uneaten parts of fruits or vegetables, grass clippings, twigs, and dead leaves in a pile moistened with water. Over time, the pile breaks down, and you will end up with a rich natural fertilizer called compost. Don't worry—compost doesn't smell like rotten food. It just smells like dirt! Adding compost to your soil helps plants grow and also allows your soil to hold more water, so you won't need to use as much water for gardening or keeping your lawn green. If you don't have a backyard, you can buy or make a compost bin.

Lisa collects soil samples from a wetland in Northern California.

"This field of coastal carbon management is really new. It's like shining a light on something that nobody was paying attention to before."

It takes about two to five weeks to make compost indoors. Then you can add compost to potted plants or donate it to a school garden, community garden, or farm. Composting reduces the waste that ends up in landfills, which produce the greenhouse gas methane. And composting makes soil richer, so plants grow better—it's a win-win!

Balancing Out Pollution with Conservation

Some companies use too many fossil fuels but are not ready to switch to using only renewable energy. These companies can balance out their carbon use by doing something to help fight climate change. Sometimes this is voluntary. Other times, the government requires the companies to contribute. Companies using too much carbon may balance out their pollution by paying to help restore a forest or by investing money in a wind-power project. You may hear the terms *carbon market* and *carbon offset* to describe this system. Lisa hopes that wetlands will become a key part of the carbon market soon. Then, if a company needs to balance out their fossil fuel use, they could pay to restore a marsh or to plant seagrass beds off the coast.

Food waste is a major issue in the United States. Composting food scraps instead of throwing them in the trash keeps that waste out of landfills.

SHAHZEEN ATTARI

Growing up in Dubai, in the United Arab Emirates, Shahzeen (Shaz) Attari saw her home transform from a beautiful desert into a busy city with tall skyscrapers and large shopping malls. She says, "I got to experience a lot of change really fast." After Shaz witnessed firsthand how much humans can negatively affect the environment, she carried that memory with her as she studied engineering in college. Later, Shaz began to study **psychology**, looking at how people view natural resources like energy and water and how they make decisions related to those resources. She also studies how to motivate people to change behaviors that are contributing to the climate crisis.

PSYCHOLOGY: the science of how people think and behave

One big question Shaz focuses on is this: **How can we convince people to act on climate change?**

Several years ago, at a conference on climate change, a man told Shaz he wouldn't listen to her ideas because she had flown to the conference on an airplane. Airplane flights are a large contributor to climate change, so the man felt that he couldn't trust Shaz as a climate expert. Shaz decided to study how a climate scientist's personal carbon footprint affects whether people will listen to that scientist. She found that if a climate expert is known to have an energy-efficient home, does not fly too much, and limits the amounts of meat they eat, people are more likely to listen to that expert, change their own home energy use, and support policies the expert recommends to address climate change. On the other hand, people are less likely to listen to an expert who is known to use a lot of fossil fuels and frequently eats meat. Although Shaz does fly occasionally, she tries to have a low carbon footprint. If she needs to fly to a conference, she might schedule another talk nearby in order to make the best use out of her airline flight. She also eats vegetarian food, composts, and has an energy-efficient home.

Shaz understands that many people see climate change as a problem that is too large to solve. When people think they can't make a difference, they don't even try. However, Shaz points to the COVID-19 pandemic as a time when people around the world made big changes quickly. Adults began to work from home, kids began to attend virtual school at home, and people of all ages began wearing masks every day. Shaz wants everyone

Shahzeen loves spending time outdoors in places such as Yellowstone National Park.

"We need to activate people rather than make them feel like the problem is too big for them to solve it."

Shahzeen regularly shares her research with all kinds of audiences.

to see the COVID-19 pandemic as a reminder that humans are capable of making significant changes. She says, "There are ways we can solve big problems like climate change if we put our minds and hearts to it, and we need strong governmental policies to address the problem."

RECOMMENDATIONS FROM SHAZ'S WORK

Climate scientists should lead by example, reducing their own carbon footprint. Equally important, climate scientists need to communicate that there *are* ways we can solve climate change. We need everyone to know it isn't too late to make a difference.

WHAT *YOU* CAN DO

You can lead by example, too, in your home, school, and community. If you make changes to reduce your carbon footprint, such as riding a bike to a friend's house instead of asking for a ride in a car or suggesting your family cook a vegetarian meal together, your siblings, parents, and classmates may begin to follow your lead. Talk with them about climate change and the actions you are taking to make a difference.

How Much Do Airplanes Contribute to Climate Change?

Most airplanes run on fossil fuels. One round-trip flight from the United States to England can release the same amount of carbon emissions as heating a home for a whole year. If you compare taking a train or a plane between the same two cities, taking a plane releases more than double the emissions per passenger. While it is possible to fly small planes using electric power, right now we don't have the technology to have large planes fly long distances using electric power. Some airlines are starting to use sustainable fuels made from used cooking oil and other waste products, and in the future more airplanes will be able to run using other climate-friendly technologies. Until then, people should consider taking fewer flights and taking trains rather than planes when possible.

The Economics of Climate Change
RIC COLACITO

Ric Colacito grew up in Italy, and he wanted to be a soccer player. But in high school, Ric noticed that Italy was going through a lot of changes related to how people spent their money and what jobs people could find. He says, "That's when I started to develop an interest in how **economics** works . . . [and] started to think of myself as possibly becoming an **economist** one day." Years later, Ric became interested in the relationship between climate change and economics.

One of the big questions Ric works on is this: How do rising temperatures affect the **economy**?

When Ric and his colleagues started their work, many people thought that climate change would only be a problem for countries where farming is the main part of the economy. They thought that climate change would not cause economic problems for countries such as the United States, where farming is just one of many industries.

But Ric found that rising temperatures *are* causing economic problems for the United States, especially in the South, where temperatures were already higher than in northern states. As expected, Ric and his colleagues found that climate change

ECONOMY: how people make money and spend money in a certain city, state, or country

ECONOMICS: the study of the economy. People have a lot of different needs (such as food and water) and wants (such as toys and fancy dresses). Economics is the study of how a society tries to meet people's needs and wants.

ECONOMIST: a scientist who studies the economy. Economists study how goods (items such as shoes and cars) and services (such as medical care and firefighting) are made, sold, and used.

"Beliefs change very slowly. But that should not be a reason for not trying."

is having a negative effect on farming. However, they found that rising temperatures are also having a negative effect on many other parts of the economy, including real estate, insurance, and car sales.

Usually, the United States economy gets bigger every year. This is measured by the gross domestic product (GDP), which is the total value of goods and services produced in a year. Ric and his colleagues figured out that if temperatures continue to rise over the next one hundred years, the GDP might stop growing as fast as normal. This could make it harder for people to find jobs.

When Ric first tried to share this work, some scientific journals told him that his findings were not important enough to publish. But since then, newspapers, banks, insurance companies, and government leaders have all seen and shared his research. Ric hopes that by providing "evidence and science and facts about the things that have already occurred and the risks we're likely to face going forward," more and more people will realize how crucial it is to take action against climate change.

RECOMMENDATIONS FROM RIC'S WORK

If citizens and policy makers understand how much rising temperatures will hurt the economy, they may be more willing to make personal changes and policy changes to limit climate change. Ric believes we need to keep pressure on businesses. He says, "Forcing companies to disclose more and more information about how much they are polluting and the steps they're taking to pollute less and less going forward, that's important."

In addition to studying the economy, Ric also teaches economics classes.

"Hopefully the small role each of us plays in gathering evidence is providing more and more tools for politicians and policy makers as a whole to start taking action."

WHAT *YOU* CAN DO

Think about what restaurants you eat in or what brand of shoes you buy. You are supporting those companies by spending money on their products. Research the companies, and see if they are making changes to use fewer fossil fuels or less plastic or taking other steps to help fight climate change. One way to do this is to check if a company is Climate Neutral Certified. You can also search for the company name and the word *sustainability* to see if they have a public statement about their efforts. If the companies you buy products from are not making changes to help fight climate change, you can put pressure on those companies to take positive steps, such as buying carbon offsets or switching to renewable energy sources, by writing letters or emails. The email addresses of many company CEOs (chief executive officers, the leaders of companies) can be found at www.ceoemail.com. If you prefer writing a letter, you can call the company's customer service number and ask for the best mailing address to use. You can also research which companies *are* doing a good job helping fight climate change and support those companies by buying their products instead.

More Than Just Farming!

Ric and his colleagues found that warmer summer temperatures will have a negative effect on farming as well as other outdoor industries, such as forestry and fishing. However, the negative effect on those outdoor industries can spill over into other areas, such as retail food services, including grocery stores. Ric's research found that many different industries would be affected by higher temperatures, including the auto industry (production at automobile manufacturing plants drops when temperatures are over 90°F [32°C]) and the real estate industry (people may stay inside in hot weather, rather than go house shopping). Higher temperatures may also result in increased hospitalizations. In hot weather, people may need to be hospitalized due to heatstroke and heat exhaustion, and heat also increases the chance of hospitalization from chronic health conditions such as diabetes and heart disease. The increase in hospitalizations in warmer weather is bad for the health insurance industry, which has to pay most of the costs for hospital stays.

Growing Meat in a Lab
NATALIE RUBIO

Whenever she went grocery shopping with her parents in elementary school, Natalie Rubio avoided the meat section. Pigs were her favorite animal, and she couldn't wrap her head around how or why pigs became ham and bacon. In high school, Natalie became a vegetarian. In college, she learned more about how animals are raised for meat. Natalie also learned that she could use science to help farm animals, and she started searching for a career that would allow her to do that.

Now, as a **cellular agriculture** researcher, one big question Natalie works to figure out is this: How can we grow meat from **cells** so that we do not need to raise animals for meat?

Raising animals for meat contributes to climate change in two ways. First, cows and sheep produce a lot of methane when they burp and pass gas. Second, forests, which naturally pull carbon out of the air, are often cut down to clear spaces to raise or feed cows and sheep. But Natalie is searching for more climate-friendly and animal-friendly ways to produce meat. Natalie jokes that she is a "cell farmer." In her lab, researchers start with individual animal cells, which can be taken painlessly from animals, and use those cells to grow pieces of meat. Usually, **cultured meat** is grown using cells from cows, pigs, or chickens. However, Natalie and her colleagues are also trying to grow meat from insect cells, which are cheaper and easier to grow than cells from animals. Cultured meat begins with just a small number of cells, but those first cells divide over and over, creating more and more cells, and eventually produce a piece of meat.

CELL: the tiniest unit that can live on its own. The human body is made up of trillions of cells.

CELLULAR AGRICULTURE: the industry and the science behind taking products that are traditionally created through agriculture (farming) and creating them with cells instead

CULTURED MEAT: meat made by growing cells in a lab

When Natalie grows meat in the lab, she starts with a scaffold, which is a structure that the cells will grow on. The scaffold can be made out of protein from soybeans, fungus, or almost any other material that is safe to eat. The cells grow on the scaffold, and the final meat product gets its shape from that scaffold. If you want the cultured meat to have a structure similar to a steak, you start with one scaffold shape. If you want the meat to look like a chicken drumstick, you start with a different scaffold shape.

Cultured meat is starting to be available in restaurants in some countries. Natalie predicts that over the next twenty years, there will be a "slow build" with more cultured meat products becoming available. First, we may see burgers that are mainly vegetarian but with a little bit of lab-grown animal fat to make them taste more like animal burgers. Then we may see steaks grown in the lab from cow cells. Once people are used to the idea of cultured meat, and have "opened their minds a little bit," as Natalie says, we may start to see meat grown from insect cells. Meat grown from insect cells might sound yucky at first, but Natalie believes it can actually look and taste just like the meats we are used to. Someday, further in the future, humans may forget that meat ever came from farm animals!

Growing Meat for Pet Food

Household pets don't drive cars or cut down forests, but they still contribute to climate change. One scientist estimated that dogs and cats are responsible for up to 64 million tons (58 million t) of greenhouse gases entering the atmosphere every year—just from the foods they eat. Vegetarian pet foods are available. But some pets crave the taste of meat. Natalie works as a consultant for a pet food company that is using meat grown in a lab to make its pet food. She points out that growing meat for pet food isn't as complicated as growing meat for humans because you don't need to grow a whole steak or make the meat look appealing. Pet food companies can focus less on looks and more on nutrition.

RECOMMENDATIONS FROM NATALIE'S WORK

Natalie says that cultured meat has a lot of potential to help fight climate change, if we can find the best methods to produce large quantities of cultured meat to replace farm-raised meat. However, she says, "we need to invest time, energy, and talent into developing the technology."

WHAT *YOU* CAN DO

One of the reasons that scientists are working to grow meat in a lab is because it is hard for people to change their behavior. Cultured meat could allow people to keep eating the same meats that they enjoy, except "in a more sustainable way." But in the meantime, Natalie says it is helpful if people eat less meat—even a little bit less! Your family could taste test a few different brands of meatless burgers and see which one you like best. Or you and your friends could make a list of meatless lunch ideas, such as hummus and pita chips, or pasta salad. If you have a pet, you could also look into vegetarian pet food options.

"We need to attack climate change from all directions."

In Natalie's lab, scientists work on a variety of different projects related to cellular agriculture, often collaborating and discussing one another's results.

Discovering New Materials for New Technologies
SOSSINA HAILE

MATERIALS SCIENTIST:
someone who studies the chemistry, structure, and properties of materials used in everything around us, from bridges to cell phones

In elementary school, Sossina Haile enjoyed math and science. And Sossina knew that when she grew up, she wanted to do something to "have a positive impact on the world." As she trained to become a scientist, Sossina still wanted to do something useful, but she wasn't sure exactly what. Sossina first worked on problems related to medical care. But when she began doing research on batteries, Sossina realized she had found a way to help with the huge problem of climate change.

One of the big questions Sossina looks at in her research is this: How can we make better technologies to fight climate change?

As a **materials scientist**, Sossina strives to find better materials to use in new technologies. One type of technology that Sossina works on is called a fuel cell. A fuel cell is like a battery, except that it can *make* electricity instead of just storing electricity. A solar panel can generate electricity only when the sun shines. But if a solar panel is connected to a fuel cell, the energy from the sun can be stored and then used to make electricity even when the sun isn't shining.

Sossina and her team discovered a new material that makes fuel cells work better. Right now, some fuel cells work at a high temperature and don't last very long. Or they work at room temperature and are not very efficient. Sossina's lab found a new ceramic material that lets fuel cells work at a medium temperature. Sossina compares this medium temperature to Baby Bear's porridge in "Goldilocks and the Three Bears." Like the porridge, the new material lets fuel cells work at a temperature that is not too hot and not too cold. This way, the fuel cell can be efficient *and* last a long time.

Sossina says, "The things we do in the laboratory are long-term." This means that it usually takes years from when scientists invent something to when people everywhere can use that new invention. A company cofounded by one of Sossina's students has been working for almost ten years on making their new fuel cells into a product it can sell. While fuel cells and other new technologies will help our planet in the future, Sossina believes we also need other immediate solutions. She says until better technologies are widely available we need to pursue better government policies to "bridge the gap."

RECOMMENDATIONS FROM SOSSINA'S WORK

When Sossina's lab first discovered the new material, they weren't planning to use it for fuel cells. Only after they created it and studied it did they realize it could be used for that purpose.

Reversible Fuel Cells

One type of fuel cell Sossina works on is a reversible fuel cell, which has two modes. In one mode, used when the sun is shining, the fuel cell takes electricity generated from solar panels and uses it to break water apart into hydrogen and oxygen. In the other mode, when there's no sunlight, the fuel cell takes the hydrogen created by breaking apart water and uses it to make electric power.

"Happy accidents" like this happen frequently in scientific research. The medicine penicillin was also discovered by accident. As scientists work to create new technologies, they should keep in mind that a product created for one purpose may end up having a different role in the fight against climate change.

WHAT *YOU* CAN DO

The materials Sossina creates in her lab will be useful in fighting climate change. But before these new technologies are widely available, Sossina says, "Society needs to keep the pressure up" and push our government to make policy changes that can have "near-term impacts." That's something you can help with! Write to your mayor, your governor, your senators, and your representatives in Congress. Tell them you want them to pass climate-friendly policies. Or plan a postcard-writing party, where you and your friends write postcards together and mail them to your local officials.

MARK JACOBSON

In middle school, Mark Jacobson visited Los Angeles and San Diego, California, for several tennis tournaments. During each visit, he saw the air pollution and thought, "Why do people have to live like this?" In college, Mark wanted to study air pollution to learn how to help fix the problem he had observed. But, he says, "There was no degree that I could do on air pollution or anything like it." So Mark studied all the related subjects he could find, including math, physics, and environmental engineering. Finally, in graduate school, Mark had the chance to specifically study air pollution. Today, as an **atmospheric and energy scientist**, Mark is still studying how we can reduce pollution.

One of the big questions Mark researches is this: How can we stop using fossil fuels to power buildings and vehicles and instead use 100 percent renewable energy?

Mark studies air pollution, such as the black, powdery substance called soot that is left when a material is not completely burned, using a **computer model**. Mark's model analyzes both weather and pollution, and how they affect each other. The model is three-dimensional, which means that it breaks up the atmosphere into little cubes and analyzes the soot, carbon dioxide, and other gases and particles in each "cube" of atmosphere. Using this model, Mark discovered that soot traps a lot of heat in our atmosphere. In fact, soot contributes to global warming and climate change more than any other chemical except carbon dioxide.

Mark believes that the whole world should stop using fossil fuels, which produce both carbon dioxide and soot. Instead, he thinks we should only use renewable energy from wind, water, and

ATMOSPHERIC AND ENERGY SCIENTIST: someone who studies Earth's atmosphere and how the way we get energy from fossil fuels, solar power, and other sources affects the atmosphere

COMPUTER MODEL: a computer program designed to show, or simulate, what might happen in a certain situation

sunlight (WWS). Mark and his colleagues have developed plans to show how each of the fifty US states could switch over to 100 percent renewable energy. He has also developed plans for individual cities and for 145 countries, showing how they could switch to WWS. For example, it might be best for a city in sunny Florida to use mostly solar power, while a city in windy South Dakota might get more power from wind.

Mark's own house is powered by solar panels. Not only is Mark's house more sustainable, but he does not need to pay an electric bill, a natural gas bill, or even a gasoline bill for his car. That's because he can charge his electric car with the solar panels too. Mark's solar panels generate more electricity than he needs to power everything in his house. The electricity he doesn't need goes back to the electrical grid, and electrical companies pay Mark for that extra electricity. Mark thinks all new houses should be built to use 100 percent renewable energy. The government can help by giving money to builders who construct houses in this way. Mark says, "If I can do it, everybody can do it."

RECOMMENDATIONS FROM MARK'S WORK

Mark believes that moving the whole world to WWS is the best way to fight climate change and that it *is* possible to do. He says, "We have the resources. We have the ability. We have the know-how. It's just a question of doing it."

WHAT *YOU* CAN DO

Research solar panel options in your community. Look for programs where solar panels are installed for free or where people can get money back from the government for installing solar panels on their homes or apartment buildings. You may find local programs that allow people to switch to solar energy and actually save money in the process! You can start your research here: www.energy.gov /eere/solar/homeowners-guide -going-solar. After you finish researching, spread the word about what you find out to your family, your neighbors, and other people in your community.

"Focus on what works and keep a positive attitude, because we *can* solve the problem."

Mark's solar panels provide the electricity for his cars as well as his house. He has a charging station in his garage.

How Do Solar Panels on a House Work?

Solar panels change energy from the sun into electrical energy. Solar panels are made of lots of little units called photovoltaic (PV) cells. Photovoltaic means that these units can turn sunlight into electricity. If you look closely at a battery, you can see there is a positive (+) end and a negative (-) end. Similarly, PV cells have positive and negative layers, which form an electric field. When sun shines on a solar panel, the PV cells absorb the light energy and generate an electric current. This electric current (direct current) is converted into the right type of electricity (alternating current) to power the home.

New Fuels to Fight Climate Change
CORINNE SCOWN

Corinne Scown remembers visiting national parks with her family when she was a kid, taking part in Junior Ranger programs that involved cleaning up trash. "That taught me how important it is to protect the environment," she says. Corinne also visited her dad's chemistry lab and saw how exciting it was to be a scientist. After considering a career as a violinist, Corinne decided to become a **civil engineer**, working on problems related to climate change.

One big question Corinne focuses on in her work is this: How can we make sure that new technologies are actually good for the environment?

CIVIL ENGINEER: someone who works on designing or building things related to transportation

BIOFUELS: fuels made out of plants, algae, or animal dung

BIOPRODUCTS: products, such as laundry detergent or plastic, that are made out of plants, algae, or animal dung

Right now, most cars, trucks, and airplanes use gas that comes from fossil fuels. Most plastics that we use are also produced from fossil fuels. Scientists are working to develop **biofuels** and **bioproducts** that are not made from fossil fuels to use instead. However, they have to make sure that these new products are better for the environment than the products they are replacing. "Just because something is 'bio' doesn't mean it's better," Corinne explains.

Recently, Corinne's team has been trying to develop **drought-resistant** crops to use in producing biofuels. They are using sorghum, a grain crop that is naturally drought resistant and continues to grow well as climate change causes more droughts. Corinne's team is experimenting with growing a new type of sorghum that would break down more easily when making biofuels.

DROUGHT-RESISTANT: able to survive even in times when water is scarce

Corinne (*center*) and her team look at one of their experimental plots of sorghum, which can be used to make biofuels.

Why Are Biofuels (Sometimes) Better for the Planet Than Fossil Fuels?

When we burn fossil fuels, such as coal, carbon dioxide goes into the atmosphere and traps heat. This leads to global warming and climate change. Burning biofuels releases carbon dioxide into the atmosphere too. However, plants grown for biofuels also pull carbon dioxide *out* of the atmosphere. While biofuels *can* be more climate-friendly than fossil fuels, it is important to think about how the biofuels are produced. For example, if pesticides and fertilizers are used when plants are grown for biofuels, those chemicals can wash into nearby bodies of water. That is why scientists should complete a life cycle assessment for all new biofuels to make sure they are better for the environment than a fossil fuel.

"There are so many good places to start. You just have to pick some and move as quickly as you can."

Once a new biofuel or bioproduct is created, Corinne performs a life cycle assessment. She studies how a new product is produced, how it would be used, and what would happen to the product when it can't be used anymore—such as whether it can be recycled. Sometimes, Corinne will analyze a new product and suggest that the scientists who created it make a change to make the product more environmentally friendly. Other times, she will tell those scientists they need to start over, because the bioproduct is harmful to the environment.

Making a biofuel involves many steps. These include coming up with an idea, testing it, and assessing the environmental impacts. The last step is scaling up, which means building factories to produce the biofuel in large quantities. But Corinne says there are biofuels that we can scale up right now. She adds, "We just have to get started. If we debate what is the ideal solution for too long, we will run out of time." While Corinne has cared deeply about climate change for years, these days she thinks about what kind of climate we will have when her young children are adults. She says, "It gives me a new sense of urgency."

RECOMMENDATIONS FROM CORINNE'S WORK

We need to scale up the environmentally friendly biofuels we have now, even if they are not perfect. We also need to work on the ones that are still

Corinne and her colleague are holding samples of their new plastics, which can be recycled an infinite number of times. Most plastics can only be recycled a few times, if they can be recycled at all.

being developed—the ones that are still five years (or more) away from being ready to use.

WHAT *YOU* CAN DO

Right now, we're years away from using biofuels and bioproducts on a large scale. So you can help by trying to limit your use of traditional fuels and plastics. Some ways to do this would be walking or riding your bike whenever possible, instead of riding in a car, and skipping single-use plastics. When you bring your lunch to school, choose a refillable water bottle and a reusable sandwich wrap or container.

"No one solution is going to solve all our problems, but we know where to start."

RYAN EMANUEL

Whether exploring the Lumbee River with his cousins or attending church with his parents and brother, Ryan Emanuel grew up feeling a strong connection to his family's tribe, the Lumbee. Ryan loved spending time outside as a kid, especially on the water. He also enjoyed studying science in school. When Ryan found out that a **hydrologist** gets to jump into rivers and also do calculations and solve problems, he knew it was the right job for him. Today, Ryan studies questions related to water and climate. He also works to amplify voices of Indigenous communities, including the Lumbee.

One big question Ryan considers is this: As we adapt to a changing climate, how can we make sure **adaptation** is respectful to all communities?

Around the world, rising sea levels and extreme weather events caused by climate change are forcing people to leave their homes. The Lumbee have been hit with both floods and droughts in recent years. Ryan explains that moving away from your home is difficult for anyone, but for Indigenous communities it can be more complicated. Ryan says, "Part of our identity comes from being able to live in the same place that our ancestors lived, see the same wetlands, use the same traditional materials and plants. If we have to leave that behind because of climate change, it severs ties with part of our identity."

Ryan works with Native American communities, listens to their ideas about how to adapt to climate change, and uses his knowledge as a hydrologist to help their solutions succeed. Right now, he is collaborating on a project with the Coharie Tribe. They are working to restore and protect the Coharie River and to turn it into an ecotourism destination. Ryan helps them monitor water levels and water quality and figure out how floods and droughts will affect the river.

Ryan helped install this weather station on a farm in Honduras. This device will measure wind, rainfall, and temperature in the area.

Another project Ryan works on involves *ghost forests*, which are forests of dead trees, such as those along the North Carolina coast. When salt water from the ocean creeps into the land, during dry periods or storms, it kills the trees in its path. Ryan identifies which coastal lands might become ghost forests in the future and advises on how to stop that from happening. These lands are hard to protect from rising sea levels, but Ryan says, "All places are worth fighting for."

What Is Ecotourism?

Ecotourism is a type of tourism in which people are welcomed to visit a natural area in a way that is good for the environment and benefits the local people. The visit often includes an education component. When ecotourism works well, it has minimal impact on the area, generates money for conservation, and provides positive experiences for both hosts and visitors. Would you like to go whale watching, or zip-lining through the rain forest? These types of experiences can be examples of ecotourism, such as a whale-watching company that educates visitors about whales and uses the money they make toward whale research, ocean conservation programs, and supporting local communities.

RECOMMENDATIONS FROM RYAN'S WORK

For thousands of years, Indigenous communities in the western United States carried on an ancient tradition of controlled burns to clear out underbrush in forests. After state authorities prohibited the Native communities from conducting this practice, overgrown forests allowed wildfires to spread more quickly. Now, government officials are beginning to see the value of cultural burns. They are reaching out to Indigenous leaders to learn from and partner with them. As we adapt to climate change, we need to listen to all communities that are affected, both to benefit from knowledge each community brings to the table and to shape adaptation measures around what the communities want for themselves.

WHAT *YOU* CAN DO

A big part of Ryan's job is listening to others, making sure everyone feels heard and valued. You can share what you know about climate change with your family, your classmates, and your community. You can also *listen* to people from other communities when they are willing to share with you their knowledge and experiences related to climate change. If a hurricane or heat wave hits the area where you live, are all communities affected in the same way?

Ryan climbs a 100-foot (30 m) tower in the Blue Ridge Mountains to check on equipment that measures the amount of carbon dioxide in the atmosphere.

"We can't just give up. We can't just abandon places that are important to our cultures and to our histories. Whether we are Native people or whether we have other backgrounds, all places are worth fighting for."

NATASHA DEJARNETT

Natasha DeJarnett, Ph.D.
Division of Cardiovascular Medicine
Department of Medicine

When Natasha DeJarnett was a young child, she traveled from her home in Kentucky to visit relatives in Birmingham, Alabama. When she arrived, Natasha had trouble breathing. She didn't know why. Years later, as a scientist trained in **public health**, Natasha understands that poor air quality in her grandparents' neighborhood in Birmingham made it hard for her to breathe. Natasha also knows that air quality is affected by many factors, including climate change, and that people of color are more likely to live in areas with poor air quality.

One big question Natasha studies is this: How is climate change negatively affecting health, and what can we do to help people who are affected?

PUBLIC HEALTH: the health of a city, country, or population as a whole

Climate change causes heat waves, and heat waves cause **cardiovascular disorders**, breathing problems, and other health issues. Natasha studies the way climate change affects public health and tries to help politicians and decision makers make better choices about what to do when there is a heat wave. For example, some cities open cooling centers, which are places where people can go to cool down. But Natasha looks at **interventions** such as cooling centers and asks, "Are there any populations that don't benefit?" In the case of cooling centers, if they're accessible only by car, people who do not have cars cannot get there to cool down. Politicians need to make sure cooling centers are located near public transportation so that everyone has access.

Natasha also studies the health value of planting trees in cities. In many cities, people of color live in neighborhoods that do not have many trees. The air quality in these neighborhoods is poor compared to neighborhoods with more trees, and climate change makes the air quality even worse. But when cities plant more trees, air quality, heart and lung health, and mental health all improve.

Trees also help neighborhoods cool down faster during heat waves.

In the past, messages about climate change focused on shrinking ice caps and the dangers to polar bears and other Arctic animals. Natasha points out, "These messages can make climate change feel very far away, both mentally and physically." Her research helps show that the dangers of climate change are not just in the Arctic but in our own neighborhoods and our own bodies. Natasha says, "Climate change is affecting health today. Right now."

RECOMMENDATIONS FROM NATASHA'S WORK

We need to clearly communicate to everyone, including politicians and decision makers, that climate change affects human health and that it is

CARDIOVASCULAR DISORDERS: illnesses or medical conditions related to the heart and blood vessels

INTERVENTION: when the government does something to try to help in a certain situation, such as opening up shelters when people have to evacuate an area due to wildfires or flooding

affecting our health right now. We should share this message—and the scientific data that support it—in newspapers, magazines, books, and movies, through social media, on the radio and on TV. People who see climate change as a future problem or don't think they are interested in climate change may be motivated to act if they realize their own health and the health of their family is already being affected.

WHAT *YOU* CAN DO

You can help plant trees in your community to improve health and cooling. If you have a yard, you can plant trees there. You can ask your school about planting trees on the school grounds. And you can encourage your city to become part of Arbor Day Foundation's Tree City USA program (www.arborday.org /programs/treecityusa/). You can also help spread the message that climate change is affecting your health, your family's health, and your community's health and that we need to start making changes now, not later.

"Sharing the story that climate change is a threat to health can build bridges. You say 'climate change' to people who are not interested in climate change and their eyes glaze over. But health can be a bridge. Many people care about health. They care about the health of themselves and their families."

Natasha measures a man's blood pressure at a community event.

How Do Trees Help Cities Stay Cool?

First, trees help cities stay cool by providing shade. In shady communities, the air and the buildings don't get as hot as the air and buildings in sunny areas. And trees also help cities cool down in another way, called evapotranspiration. When the sun's rays hit a tree's leaves, water evaporates from the leaves. As the liquid water turns into gas (water vapor), it cools the surrounding air.

HOW CAN *YOU* BE A CLIMATE WARRIOR?

Just as the scientists in this book are tackling the problem of climate change in different ways, there are lots of different ways kids and teenagers can help fight climate change. How you decide to help will depend on your abilities and interests, but any way you can help is important. If everyone contributes a little, those efforts add up to big changes.

Here is a list of some things you can do to help fight climate change:

- **Reducing plastics.** You can switch to reusable containers instead of plastic bags for your lunch or leftover food and encourage your family to use refillable water bottles and soap dispensers, instead of single-use plastics.

- **Reducing waste that ends up in landfills.** You can sew a button back on your favorite shirt instead of buying a new one and donate outgrown toys instead of throwing them away. You can also shop for clothes in thrift stores, rather than buying brand-new clothes.

- **Being mindful about water use.** You can take short showers instead of baths, turn off the faucet when you brush your teeth, and collect rainwater for watering plants.

- **Reducing energy use.** You can choose to open a window in warm weather instead of turning on the air-conditioning, put on a sweater in cold weather instead of turning up the heat, and ride your bike to a friend's house instead of asking for a ride in a car. When you need to drive to a sports practice or band rehearsal, you can try to arrange a carpool with friends instead of everyone driving in separate cars.

- **Gardening.** You can plant a butterfly garden, a rain garden, or a vegetable garden, any of which will naturally reduce the carbon dioxide in the air as well as provide other benefits. You can also participate in tree-planting efforts in your community.

- **Composting.** You can reduce waste and improve the quality of soil by turning food scraps and fallen leaves into fertilizer. If you have a backyard, you can start a compost pile there and use the finished compost to fertilize your yard. Some cities have compost drop-off locations where you can bring your collected food scraps.

- **Choosing sustainable foods.** You can eat less meat, especially beef and lamb. You can also look for farmers markets or community-supported agriculture (CSA) programs in your area. Buying foods grown nearby uses a lot less fuel to get the foods to you.

- **Sharing.** You can share bikes, toys, books, and art supplies with your siblings, friends, and neighbors instead of each kid having their own. Sharing means fewer factories needed to produce these items, and fewer items ending up in landfills.

- **Using your voice.** You can talk to your school principal, or write a letter to your local government, with your ideas for making climate-friendly changes. You can also join a climate rally, where you make a poster and march with others to show the government how many people care about fighting climate change.

WORKING TOGETHER

The scientists in this book work in different fields. They don't know one another. But they are still working together, because they are all trying their best to fight climate change. Other scientists, from chemists to meteorologists to geologists, are tackling this problem too. These scientists might work in labs, under the ocean, or even in Antarctica! But they all have the same goals: to find ways to slow down climate change and to adapt to the changes that have already occurred.

Certain things we can do to address climate change are big, such as constructing net-zero buildings that do not release any extra carbon dioxide into the atmosphere. Some things are small, such as wearing an older sibling's hand-me-down jeans even if you would rather buy new ones. But we need the big changes *and* the small changes.

Although climate change is the largest environmental challenge humans have ever faced, we can't start thinking that climate change is too big of a problem to solve. We can't give up and say, "No matter what we do, it won't make a difference." We need to make little changes on our own. We need to team up to make larger changes. We need to keep talking about climate change until *everybody* understands what a huge problem it is. And we need to push our elected officials to make better laws. We all need to work together as climate warriors.

Even planting a small plot in your yard or in a community garden can have a big impact.

YOUNG CLIMATE WARRIORS

People of all ages are working to save our planet. Meet a few young climate warriors from around the world:

Fernanda Barros, Brazil

Fernanda Barros is worried about the future of the Amazon rainforest and the Indigenous people who live there. In the past few years, the government of Brazil has removed environmental protections for the rainforest. At the age of sixteen, Fernanda cofounded Fridays for Future Amazonia, a branch of the global organization Fridays for Future, which was started by Greta Thunberg. Barros wants to make sure that the climate movement listens to youth Amazonian voices. Many people around the world see the Amazon rainforest as an important part of fighting climate change because of its rich biodiversity and its capacity to absorb lots of carbon dioxide from the atmosphere. But Barros believes it is important for leaders and scientists to hear the opinions and ideas of the young people who call the Amazon rainforest home.

Lesein Mutunkei, Kenya

When he was twelve years old, Lesein learned that cutting down forests is a huge problem in his country. He decided to take something he loves, soccer, and combine it with activism. He started Trees for Goals to plant eleven trees for each goal he scored (one tree for each of the eleven players on a soccer team). Lesein began reaching out to schools and soccer clubs to get others to join in his efforts. More than fourteen hundred trees have been planted so far, primarily in urban forests in Nairobi, Kenya.

Nadia Nazar, United States

At the age of fifteen, Nadia Nazar worked with three fellow teenagers to found Zero Hour. Nadia and her cofounders were frustrated that youth voices are often ignored in climate change conversations, even though climate change will have a much bigger effect on the lives of teenagers than on the lives of their parents' generation. Zero Hour organizes young people to take action against climate change in a variety of ways, including lobbying politicians in Washington, DC, and providing training sessions for young people who want to become activists. As an artist, Nadia also believes in the power of art to help send an important message: we must take action to address climate change!

Nadia Nazar

Anjali Sharma, Australia

Anjali Sharma was sixteen when she led a lawsuit with seven other high school students against the environmental minister of Australia. Her goal was to prevent a coal mine expansion project from moving forward. Australia depends on energy from coal to power most of their industries. However, Anjali argued that the mine expansion could release over 110 million more tons (100 million t) of carbon dioxide into the air and that Australia had a responsibility to think about children in the face of the climate crisis. Although the government decided to go ahead with the coal mine expansion, Anjali continues her advocacy by writing and speaking about climate change and campaigning for climate-friendly candidates.

Greta Thunberg, Sweden

Greta Thunberg began protesting outside the Swedish Parliament House at the age of fifteen. Day after day, she sat there, holding up a School Strike for Climate sign in an attempt to convince her government to meet targets for reducing carbon emissions. Thousands of students across the globe joined Greta in skipping school to protest the lack of action on climate change by their governments. Since her strike, Greta has spoken with world leaders and given speeches at major climate change conferences, pressuring governments to commit to higher standards for reducing emissions. Greta has received multiple Nobel Peace Prize nominations for her climate activism.

Greta Thunberg

HOW TO WRITE A LETTER TO THE GOVERNMENT

Writing a letter is a small way to make a big difference. Letters written to elected officials (the people who make up the government) really do get read, and they can make a huge impact.

When you write to an elected official, the first step is to figure out what you want to say. Do you want to suggest that your city switch to electric school buses? Do you want to ask your elected official not to allow any new natural-gas power plants to open in your state?

Your next step is to figure out the best person or people to address your letter to. If you are writing about a topic that affects your whole state or the whole country, you can write to the US House representative for your district or your US senators. You can find your US senators and representative here: www.congress.gov/members /find-your-member. You can also write to the governor of your state.

If you are writing about a topic that specifically affects your city or your county, you can write to your local elected officials, such as the mayor or your county executive. You can find your local elected officials here: www.usa.gov/elected-officials.

Now, craft your letter! Here's a basic template you can follow.

Your address*:
Your email address*:
Date:

Dear _____,

My name is _____, and I am writing to you because _____ (Explain why you care about this issue. Then include facts, evidence, and examples. Be as specific as possible.).

I hope that you will _____ (Explain the actions you hope your elected official will take.).

Thank you very much for taking the time to read my letter.

Sincerely,
_____ (your signature)
_____ (your printed name)

Keep your letter short and to the point, and be polite. After you are finished writing, don't forget to read through the letter before you send it to check for any grammatical or spelling errors!

*It is common to include your contact information when writing to an elected official, and they need your contact information if you hope to receive a response. However, you should check with your parent or guardian before sending your letter about what kinds of contact information they think you should include.

GLOSSARY

atmosphere: all the gases, or air, surrounding Earth

carbon emissions: carbon dioxide produced by planes, cars, factories, and other similar sources

carbon footprint: the amount of carbon dioxide and other carbon compounds that are released into the atmosphere because of the fossil fuels used by a person or a company

data: facts, statistics, or information

drought: a weather condition when there is too little rain, causing a shortage of water

ecologist: a scientist who studies ecology, which is how organisms are related to one another and to their surroundings

ecosystem: a community of organisms interacting with one another and with their physical environment

electrical grid: an interconnected network for getting electricity from places where energy is produced, such as power plants, and delivering it to places where energy is used, such as homes, restaurants, hospitals, or offices

emissions: gases discharged into the atmosphere

fossil fuel: a natural fuel such as coal or gas, formed over millions of years from the remains of living organisms

global warming: the increase in Earth's average surface temperature due to increasing levels of greenhouse gases trapping heat in the atmosphere

greenhouse gases: gases such as carbon dioxide and methane that trap heat in the atmosphere

ice age: a period where temperatures around the globe are colder and more of Earth becomes covered by glaciers

photosynthesis: a process in which plants use sunlight to make their own food out of carbon dioxide and water

policy: a course of action that is proposed or decided upon by a government, a business, or an individual

policy maker: a person responsible for making policy, often someone in government

renewable energy: energy that can't run out, such as energy from the sun or the wind

sustainable: meeting the needs of the present without making it impossible for future generations to meet their own needs. When this word is used in the context of climate change, it usually means being good for the environment and not using too many fossil fuels.

technologies: machinery or equipment developed by applying scientific knowledge

SOURCE NOTES

10 Thomas Crowther, interview with the author, August 23, 2021.

12 Crowther.

13 Crowther.

13 Crowther.

14 Meg Holden, interview with the author, October 4, 2021.

15 Holden.

17 Holden.

17 Holden.

18 Wendy Chou, interview with the author, August 30, 2021.

19 Chou.

20 Chou.

21 Chou.

21 Chou.

21 Chou.

24 Jessi Allen, interview with the author, October 4, 2021.

24 Allen.

24 Allen.

25 Allen.

25 Allen.

25 Allen.

26 David Rolnick, interview with the author, August 18, 2021.

27 Rolnick.

28 Lisa Windham-Myers, interview with the author, September 28, 2021.

29 Windham-Myers.

29 Windham-Myers.

30 Windham-Myers.

32 Shahzeen Attari, interview with the author, July 29, 2021.

33 Attari.

34 Attari.

36 Ric Colacito, interview with the author, September 27, 2021.

37 Colacito.

37 Colacito.

38 Colacito.

38 Colacito.

41 Natalie Rubio, interview with the author, September 21, 2021.

41 Rubio.

43 Rubio.

43 Rubio.

43 Rubio.

44 Sossina Haile, interview with the author, September 6, 2021.

45 Haile.

45 Haile.

45 Haile.

46 Mark Jacobson, interview with the author, September 8, 2021.

47 Jacobson.

48 Jacobson.

48 Jacobson.

50 Corinne Scown, interview with the author, August 23, 2021.

51 Scown.

52 Scown.

52 Scown.

53 Scown.

55 Ryan Emanuel, interview with the author, August 16, 2021.

55 Emanuel.

57 Emanuel.

59 Natasha DeJarnett, interview with the author, August 3, 2021.

59 DeJarnett.

60 DeJarnett.

SELECTED BIBLIOGRAPHY

Attari, Shahzeen, David H. Krantz, and Elke U. Weber. "Climate Change Communicators' Carbon Footprints Affect Their Audience's Policy Support." *Climatic Change* 154, no. 3 (June 2019): 529–545. https://link.springer.com/article/10.1007/s10584-019-02463-0.

Bastin, Jean-François, Yelena Finegold, Claude Garcia, Danilo Mollicone, Marcelo Rezende, Devin Routh, M. Zohner, and Thomas W. Crowther. "The Global Tree Restoration Potential." *Science* 365, no. 6448 (2019): 76–79. https://www.science.org/doi/10.1126/science.aax0848.

Brown, Jessica. "Why Cellular Agriculture Could Be the Future of Farming." BBC Future (BBC), November 23, 2019. https://www.bbc.com/future/article/20211116-how-the-food-industry-might-cut-its-carbon-emissions.

Clifford, Catherine. "U.S. Can Get to 100% Clean Energy with Wind, Water, Solar, and Zero Nuclear, Stanford Professor Says." CNBC, December 21, 2021. https://www.cnbc.com/2021/12/21/us-can-get-to-100percent-clean-energy-without-nuclear-power-stanford-professor-says.html.

"Climate Change: Should You Fly, Drive or Take the Train?" BBC News, August 24, 2019. https://www.bbc.com/news/science-environment-49349566.

Colacito, Riccardo, Bridget Hoffmann, and Toan Phan. "Temperature and Growth: A Panel Analysis of the United States." *Journal of Money, Credit and Banking* 51, no. 2–3 (March/April 2019): 313–368.

Drouin, Roger. "Lichens Could Be Physically Rescued from Sea Level Rise." *Scientific American*, April 1, 2017. https://www.scientificamerican.com/article/lichens-could-be-physically-rescued-from-sea-level-rise/.

Emanuel, Kerry. *What We Know about Climate Change.* Rev. ed. Cambridge, MA: MIT University Press, 2018.

Figueres, Christiana, and Tom Rivett-Carnac. *The Future We Choose: The Stubborn Optimist's Guide to the Climate Crisis*. New York: Alfred A. Knopf, 2020.

"How Researchers Can Help Fight Climate Change in 2022 and Beyond." *Nature* 601, no. 7 (2022). https://www.nature.com/articles/d41586-021-03817-4.

Macreadie, Peter, Andrea Anton, John A. Raven, Nicola Beaumont, Rod M. Connolly, Daniel A. Friess, Jeffrey J. Kelleway et al. "The Future of Blue Carbon Science." *Nature Communications* 10, no. 3998 (2019). https://www.nature.com/articles/s41467-019-11693-w.

Mann, Michael E. "The Right Path Forward on Climate Change." *Newsweek*, February 23, 2021. https://www.newsweek.com/right-path-forward-climate-change-opinion-1571169.

Nunez, Christina. "Biofuels, Explained." *National Geographic*, July 15, 2019. https://www.nationalgeographic.com/environment/article/biofuel.

———. "Global Warming Solutions, Explained." *National Geographic*, January 24, 2019. https://www.nationalgeographic.com/environment/article/global-warming-solutions.

Reed, Stanley, and Jack Ewing. "Hydrogen Is One Answer to Climate Change. Getting It Is the Hard Part." *New York Times*, July 13, 2021. https://www.nytimes.com/2021/07/13/business/hydrogen-climate-change.html.

Rolnick, David, Priya L. Donti, Lynn H. Kaack, Kelly Kochanski, Alexandre Lacoste, Kris Sankaran, Andrew Slavin Ross et al. "Tackling Climate Change with Machine Learning." *ACM Computing Surveys* 55, no. 2 (March 2023): 1–96. https://dl.acm.org/doi/10.1145/3485128.

Schiermeier, Quirin. "Eat Less Meat: UN Climate-Change Report Calls for Change to Human Diet." *Nature* 572, no. 7769 (August 2019): 291–292. https://www.nature.com /articles/d41586-019-02409-7.

Treisman, Rachel. "How Loss of Historic Lands Makes Native Americans More Vulnerable to Climate Change." NPR, November 2, 2021. https://knpr.org/npr/2021-11 /how-loss-historical-lands-makes-native-americans -more-vulnerable-climate-change.

Yeager, Ray, Daniel W. Riggs, Natasha DeJarnett, David J. Tollerud, Jeffrey Wilson, Daniel J. Conklin, Timothy E. O'Toole et al. "Association Between Residential Greenness and Cardiovascular Disease Risk." *Journal of the American Heart Association* 7, no. 24 (December 2018): e009117. https://www.ahajournals.org/doi/10.1161/JAHA.118.009117.

FURTHER READING

Books

Davenport, Leslie. *All the Feelings Under the Sun: How to Deal with Climate Change*. Washington, DC: Magination, 2021.

Herman, Gail. *What Is Climate Change?* New York: Penguin Workshop, 2018.

Margolin, Jamie. *Youth to Power: Your Voice and How to Use It*. New York: Hachette Go, 2020.

Minoglio, Andrea. *Our World Out of Balance: Understanding Climate Change and What We Can Do*. San Francisco: Blue Dot Kids, 2021.

Thunberg, Greta. *No One Is Too Small to Make a Difference*. New York: Penguin, 2019.

Websites for Kids

Composting at Home
https://www.epa.gov/recycle/composting-home

NASA Climate Kids
https://climatekids.nasa.gov/

National Geographic Kids: Climate Change
https://kids.nationalgeographic.com/science/article /climate-change

Websites for Educators

Climate Change Resources for Educators and Students
https://www.epa.gov/climate-change/climate-change -resources-educators-and-students

National Geographic Society: Climate Change
https://www.nationalgeographic.org/education /climate-change/

INDEX

PHOTO ACKNOWLEDGMENTS

Image credits: Stockphoto/Getty Images, p. 4; OchTom/Wikipedia (CC BY-SA 4.0), p. 5; Courtesy of the National Oceanic and Atmospheric Administration Central Library Photo Collection, pp. 6, 7; Erik McGregor/LightRocket/Getty Images, p. 8; Courtesy of The Crowther Lab, pp. 10, 12; Courtesy of Meg Holden, pp. 14, 15; Ron Bedard/Alamy Stock Photo, p. 16; Courtesy of Marcus Jackson Photography, pp. 18, 20; Courtesy of Sean McKenzie, p. 22; Ed Reschke/Getty Images, p. 23; Paul Souders/Stone/Getty Images, p. 25; Courtesy of Guillaume Simoneau, p. 26; Courtesy of Jeff Myers, p. 28; Courtesy of Jacob Fleck, p. 30; Skorzewiak/Shutterstock, p. 31; Courtesy of Center for Advanced Study in the Behavioral Sciences at Stanford University, pp. 32, 35; Courtesy of Shahzeen Attari, p. 33; Courtesy of Riccardo Colacito, pp. 36, 38; djgis/Shutterstock, p. 39; Photo by Tricia Rubio, p. 40; chendongshan/iStockphoto/Getty Images, p. 42; Courtesy of New Harvest, p. 43; Courtesy of Sossina Haile, p. 44; Courtesy of Mark Jacobson, pp. 46, 48; Westend61/Getty Images, p. 49; © 2010 The Regents of the University of California, through the Lawrence Berkeley National Laboratory, pp. 50, 51, 53; Courtesy of Ryan Emanuel, pp. 54, 55, 57; Niki Harry/500 Prime/Getty Images, p. 56; Courtesy of Tom Fougerousse/University of Louisville, p. 58; Courtesy of Aria Higgins, p. 60; PapaBear/iStock/Getty Images, p. 61; Monkey Business Images/Shutterstock p. 62; SolStock/Getty Images, p. 64; AP Photo/Markus Schreibe, p. 66; Eric BARADAT/AFP/Getty Images, p. 65; ju_see/Shutterstock (backgrounds).

Front cover: Alistair Berg/Getty Images; Monkey Business Images/Shutterstock; A3pfamily/Shutterstock; ju_see/Shutterstock.